Love Lyrics

Poetry for the Heart

J. B. L.

• Chicago •

Love Lyrics
Poetry for the Heart
J. B. L.

Published by
Joshua Tree Publishing
• Chicago •
JoshuaTreePublishing.com

All rights reserved. No part of this book may be reproduced or transmitted in any form or by any means, electronic or mechanical, including information storage and retrieval system without written permission from the publisher, except by a reviewer who may quote brief passages in a review.

13-Digit ISBN: 978-1-956823-00-4
Copyright © 2021. J. B. L. All Rights Reserved.

Disclaimer:
This book is designed to provide information about the subject matter covered. The opinions and information expressed in this book are those of the author, not the publisher. Every effort has been made to make this book as complete and as accurate as possible. However, there may be mistakes both typographical and in content. Therefore, this text should be used only as a general guide and not as the ultimate source of information. The author and publisher of this book shall have neither liability nor responsibility to any person or entity with respect to any loss or damage caused or alleged to be caused directly or indirectly by the information contained in this book.

Printed in the United States of America

Dedication

To

This book is dedicated to the best teachers of love
Terry Seven
Tiberius Maximums

I love you all very much.

FOREWORD

I wrote this book from my heart some time ago as a young man in love for the first time. When I met this very special young lady, it seemed to be the most joyous love ever given to me. We taught each other about love and loving each other. We shared some very special moments together, mostly in her mother's living room, and talked for hours about life, love, and each other. I remember holding each other, sitting side by side, and looking into each other's eyes. We discussed our wants, needs, and love for each other while we spent a great deal of time listening and sharing. I will never forget what she meant to me. Knowing her made a great difference in my life.

I am lover with the desire to love with a deep passion. To this day, I especially now see the need to love. I had one failed marriage that should have lasted forever. But in most cases, equal levels of love do not exist though we hope for it. Mine is not the only marriage that has broken up or on its way out. We all look to prepare our loving relationships but are not always successful in doing so. Yet, in every chance I got, I spoke passionately and lovingly, and all I got was, "You are too melodramatic" and "You don't mean it." I'm sure you've experienced something similar. Maybe I was. But nevertheless I was honest in what I felt and said about loving this person. We may all lose at love sometimes, but we should try to never give in to its hurtful pain. Remember, as long as you say every heartfelt feeling and emotion to the one you love, the love inside of you can only get better. I now whatever happens, I can or will fall in love and get married again. Even though, I would have liked my first marriage to work out, love was not always present at the right time.

I am no better than the next when it comes to love. Yes, I get disappointed and hurt over love. But who doesn't? Get over it! I also get happy with joy when love comes my way. To me love is more than a friend. It's my companion. I have a friend who says. "You talk too much about love. You're a wimp, a sad puppy." If loving someone with a deep passion and respect makes me a wimp, then I am. As far as a sad puppy, what my friend doesn't know is puppies are not sad. They just have longing, loving eyes that say, "Hug me." "Hold me." "Give me all the affection you have to offer." And you know what? They get it. So let me be a sad puppy. Come hug me, hold me, and bring on that affection! Never be ashamed of love. Let people say whatever they want. We can't stop loving because people are afraid to be sensitive to love. Because out of you, there is love. Out of me, there is love. Out of us, there is love. And out of this book of love lyrics, there is love. Enjoy with a great possibility that each page will find its way to a part of your life's journey that loves.

INTRODUCTION

There are those who are willing to fight for love, whose heart pains for love, and who are in love with a passion to stay in love until the end. Like those who yearn for that unconditional desire to love, I see the emotion for what it is . . . love.

"I love you." These three words have inspired people to love or fall in love since the beginning of time. There have been all kinds of love—new love, old love, faithful love, untrusting love, love of pain and heartache, and love of lust and longing. Then there are those like me who loves with his all, through its ups and downs, and still praise love until the end. *Love Lyrics* is what I call a collection of all these types of love with my thoughts and my feelings relating to my experiences in describing some realities of love. I know, at times, we can all be afraid of love. This is the strongest human emotion; we have ridden the emotional roller coaster at one time or another in our lives. In this book, you will read what might be considered the many aspects of love.

Don't get me wrong. I don't believe for one minute that I have all the answers or that you will find them in this book. But read well, for one or more applies somehow or someway to you as well as myself. *Love Lyrics* may be the words you may have been looking to say to someone, to romance someone, or to tell them of the torment in which love may have left you. I believe in reading the *Love Lyrics*, you will be touched and moved. If you ever have or had love in your life, this book may give you the inspiration and comfort you feel about love to be a hopeful romantic and see that love will always come again.

Open your heart to one of the many things God asked of you, " . . . above all things, love each other as you would love yourself." Remember, falling in love is not always easy, but it's a lot of fun for the heart. Have fun reading this book and enjoy!

Table of Contents

OPEN TO LOVE	13
WHEN I LOVE YOU	14
A PROMISE OF LOVE	15
POWER OF LOVE	16
THE ESSENCE OF YOU	17
DEFENSELESS	18
LOVE TOLD ME	19
WHAT I FOUND	20
BREATHLESS	21
LOVE IS . . .	22
COMPANION FEELING	23
LOVE AT FIRST SIGHT	24
LOVE ME	25
TAKE MY LOVE	26
THE FACE OF LOVE	27
EMOTION OF LOVE	28
MY SWEET BELOVED	29
JANICE	30
ODE TO MY WIFE	31
YOUR EYES	32
YOU AND I	33
I LOVE YOU	34
IN THE MORNING	35
TAKE THE PLUNGE	36
EMPTINESS	37
DON'T GO AWAY	38
MY UNCERTAINTY	39
A DAY LATE	40
MAGICAL WORDS	41

SECOND CHANCE	42
A HURTING HEART	43
RATIONAL IN LOVE	44
I WILL LOVE AGAIN	45
LOST LOVE	46
MY SILENT LOVE	47
LETTING GO OF LOVE	48
LOVE'S LOVE	49
A SPECIAL NIGHT	50
MUTUAL LOVE	51
BETTER THAN A ROSE	52
BEAUTIFUL	53
VANITY	54
AWAKEN BY YOUR LOVE	55
MY LOVE ALWAYS	56
WHY BE TOGETHER?	57
NEED LOVE	58
I PLEDGE MY LOVE	59
A SWEET HELLO	60
A SMILE FOR YOU	61
MY OPEN LOVE	62
CONFESSION OF LOVE	63
PRICELESS	64
GIFT OF LOVE	65
MY LOVE IS YOU	66
GAME OF LOVE	67
HOW MUCH I LOVE YOU	68
A PLACE IN MY HEART	69
LET OUR LOVE SOAR	70
YOU LEFT ME	71
LOVE DREAMS	72
ONE IN A CROWD	73
WHILE YOU'RE ASLEEP	74
EROTICA	75
AFTER THE RAIN	76
NEVER STOP LOVING YOU	77
CRY	78

BEFORE IT'S TOO LATE	79
YOU WALKED IN	81
WE CAN ONLY GET BETTER	82
WHILE YOU WERE WAITING	83
LOVE IN REVERSE	84
YOU ARE MY LOVE	85
ALWAYS TOGETHER	86
GIVE TO ME	87
TOSSING MY HEART	88
A MIRROR IMAGE	89
ENCHANTING BEAUTY	90
THOSE SPECIAL MOMENTS	91
WILL YOU?	92
YOUR WAY OF LOVE	93
A MESSAGE FROM LOVE	94
ONLY ME	95
IF ONLY	96
MY VOW	97
LOVE	98
JOYOUS LOVE	99
A LOVE SONG	100
GIVE TO ME	101
REFLECTIONS	102
A LOVER'S DREAM	103
WHAT HAVE WE HERE?	104
WHAT WILL IT TAKE?	105
CAN I?	106
LET'S LOVE TOMORROW	107
ONE SWEET LOVE	108
HERE'S MY LOVE	109
LOOK WHAT YOU'VE DONE	110
FOOTSTEPS	111
LAUGHTER	112
IMAGES OF YOU	113
LOVE LYRICS	114
ROMANTIC EVENING	115
KISS ME	116

THANK YOU	117
LOVE'S INFINITY	118
LOVE BEFORE DEATH	119
ONLY IF	120
MY SIMPLE LOVE	121
I FOUND LOVE IN YOU	122
TWO KINDS OF LOVE	123
ABOUT THE AUTHOR	125

OPEN TO LOVE

We should let our hearts become one in love.

To see love,

To fall in love,

To cherish love,

To give unconditional love,

And to stay forever in love.

WHEN I LOVE YOU

When I love you . . . I'll love you forever.
With my extravagance of my seductive ways,
I'll hold you forever and surrender my thoughts to you.

When I love you I'll entice your alluring beauty to my soul,
I'll clutch my heart with every whisper of your name.

When I love you I'll thrive on cherishing each moment with you,
And give to you the rapture and ecstasy that will make you tremble all over.

When I love you,
You will know.

A PROMISE OF LOVE

Come to me and I will love you.

I will see to your every need.

I will open life love for you to taste and cherish.

I will show you the many wonders of love

And how together we will make them work for us.

I will shower you with the intimate fragrance of my perfume.

I will take your untamed heart and let it blossom into a love that is full

Of magical love, sensitive love, romantic love, and especially our love

This is the love I will give to you.

POWER OF LOVE

Have you heard about what love can do for you?
Come on, open your arm and embrace it.
Taste the love in the air.
Its aroma surrounds you.
Cherish each moment it gives to you
Feel love's tenderness all round you
Come let it arouse your thirst for love
When love touches you share its wonder
And its joy
And its passion
And it may excite you to love
Even more

THE ESSENCE OF YOU

I look upon such radiant beauty
Which my eyes has never looked upon before.
I am longing to hold your delicate ebony body in my arms.
My soul will collapse with just a mere touch.

I am in ecstasy over your sweet seductive fragrance.
Even though I thirst for your succulent lips,
I dare not say more...for your beauty lures me
To expose my passionate love for you.

DEFENSELESS

Here I am submissive to your love,
But also very fragile to it as well.
I sob at the mere thought of you.
I marvel at your beauty each day I see you.
I quiver at the sound of your sweet voice.
I am so defenseless against your love.
But yet my appetite grows for more of your love.
Let me forsake my fear of my love for you,
And give in to my intense passion for you
Let this be the day I love you

LOVE TOLD ME

Love called your name to me;
It was warm and ever so sweet.
It had a loving tenderness to it.
Love told me to love you.
To give you myself and nothing less.

Love told me to see the beauty in your eyes
As well as in your heart.
Love told me to just say hello.

WHAT I FOUND

What I found in you is all the joy we share together.

What I found in you is my mate for life.

What I found in you is a life full of loving memories.

What I found in you is the laugher to stop the pain.

What I found in you is a great appreciation for just loving you.

What I found in you is myself.

BREATHLESS

Your smile embraces me;

You caress my body like raw silk.

Your laughter fills the very essence of me;

Your touch is gentle like a quiet breeze over the waters.

You entice my stony heart into a blossoming flower.

Like a rushing river, you flood my soul with passion.

You entrap my very being . . . my soul.

You leave me breathless.

LOVE IS . . .

Love is what brought us together . . .
Love is what make us better . . .
Love is what we need to survive . . .
Love is what we do when we lay down together . . .
Love is what we do for one another . . .
Love is the very best of the both of us.

Love is our family together – always . . .
Love is what I do for you and you do for me . . .
Love is all we have that really counts
In our lives together.

COMPANION FEELING

I am feeling you all over my body.
Share all of your emotions with me.
When you cry, I weep.
When you are gloomy, I am sad.
When you are happy, I am blessed.
When you are in my arms, I love you.

When you are in your sensitive mood,
I am very responsive to your tenderness.
You are my companion in love for eternity.

LOVE AT FIRST SIGHT

I fell in love with you at my first glance.
I saw in you a seductive tenderness,
A playful smile and clownish way that could even make my tears smile.
I saw in you a strong vibrant beauty that could lift up this sad heart and love it.

I cherish the moment I met you.
I hug you and feel a loving shiver leave my body.
The tearful passion of longing to love you,
Came rushing through so emotionally to my soul.

I want to cry,
But I'll settle for a rare chance to fall deeply in love with you.
So I am . . . waiting for someone to love me like you do
For the first time

LOVE ME

Here is a hug.

Here is a kiss.

Here is my love.

Here is me confusing my love to you.

This is my final plea for our love.

Say you'll take it and not be deceitful with it.

Say you'll take it and not be hurtful with it.

Say you'll take it and not be insulting with it.

Say you'll take it and not hinder its growth.

And promise to handle it with care.

TAKE MY LOVE

Take me in your arms, keeping our love from harm.
Let us stay together for a million years of love.
Love me.
Bring to me all your dreams that you thought could never be.
So we can make the love a reality . . .
Just you and me.

Love me.
For I really need you.
I confess, I need you.
Can you feel my love for you?
Love me

THE FACE OF LOVE

So many faces of love,
But I pick your face to love.
A face of such beauty to look upon,
It lights up as a full moon that shimmers at night.

I see your lovely face as something to behold in my heart.
In this world there are so many faces to love
But I am in love with yours.

It's not just your smile or your lips or your eyes,
It is your complete sexy arousing face
That inspires me to love you.

EMOTION OF LOVE

Have you heard how much I love you?
Have seen how much I love you?
Have you felt how much I love you?
Have you seen how excited I get because I love you?

I want the world to know how deliriously in love I am with you.
I am wrapped up in the emotion of just thinking about how much I really love you.
You do have me always.
To love.

MY SWEET BELOVED

My beloved, my beloved, my sweet beloved
You are my life's treasure of love.
You hold the key not only to my heart
But to my soul as well.

My beloved it is your love that holds me where I stand today
And that is close to your heart.
If ever my eyes wept a tear, it was a tear of my love for you.

My beloved you carry my love beyond the shore of life exposing my soul.
My beloved, don't ever feel the need to go.
For I shall tell everyone of your great beauty that you have given unto me.

My sweet beloved.

JANICE

Your name alone Janice says hello with a breeze of gentleness to my heart.

Your body alone speaks with the sex appeal of a Shakespeare sonnet.

Your dark loveliness shines with the essence of a dark maple honey.

Your touch has the feel of a thousand silk sheets caressing my very soul.

Please, Janice, hold me and never let me go.

ODE TO MY WIFE

You are a blessing from god.

You are all this man needs in his life

You are my life beyond life.

You are the one that I decided to spend my life with.

You are so many things to my heart and soul,

To my very being.

You are my soul mate, my wife,

My life.

YOUR EYES

When I look into your eyes
I see love and joy.
I feel the warmth and the passion in your eyes.
I feel my heart beat with a sensation of tenderness in your eyes.

As I hold you with just one look in your eyes,
I see the stars that shine brightly in your eyes.
I know that when I look in your eyes,
I see forever in your eyes.

YOU AND I

Together we are strong,
Together we stand as one,
Together we share as one,
Together we love as one,
Together we communicate as one,
Together we build up each other,
Together we face each day as one, and as long as we stay
Together as one, we will never part.

So we shall be one love, one family, one God.

I LOVE YOU

I love you like I love waterfalls, butterflies and teardrops.

I love you like moonlight and an oceanic symphony.

I love you like rain and the morning dew.

I love you from the essence of my soul,

I love you for you.

IN THE MORNING

You are my morning breeze,
You are my morning sunshine,
You are my morning lover,
You are my morning surprise,
You are my morning tenderness,
You are my morning delight,

That is why I awake to you each morning
Stimulated by the beauty you bring to my morning.
With love.

TAKE THE PLUNGE

Let's fall in the arms of love,

In the bosom of wisdom,

In the mind of understanding,

And feel the greatest joy of our lives.

Let's fall in love together . . . forever.

EMPTINESS

My love is so empty without you.

There's no one to hold.

There is no warm hello to hear.

There is no bed to lay in to love you.

There is no you to love me.

My love is empty because I don't have you to love

Anymore.

DON'T GO AWAY

Please stay, let's try to work things out.

Please stay, that our love may last forever.

Please stay, that the tears will stop hurting me.

Please stay, that we may create a new love.

Please stay because I missed you one minute after you walked out my life.

Please stay in love with me if you care at all.

Love me and stay.

MY UNCERTAINTY

To the woman I love so,
I fear your love inside me.
I stand back from your love because I'm not sure of it.
I know that my mistrust lingers about my mind and it disturbs even me.
Why do I carry my love to a dark place?

I love you.
But what I feel or what I see makes me withdraw from you.
My uncertainty will have me to lose your love.
I shall empty out my fare and love you any way.
I will deliver my love to you without hesitation.
Because I love you so.

A DAY LATE

Why now the candlelight?

Why now the romantic poem?

Why now the constant phone calls?

Why now the flowers?

Why now the "I love you"?

When love is gone what good are these things now?

If you would have shared you feelings of love always,

My love would never have let you go.

MAGICAL WORDS

What are the magic words that will put our love back together?

Is it please?
Is it forgive me?
Is it I am sorry?
Is it that won't happen again?
Is it we still love each other?
Is it I can't live without you?
Or just I love you?

I will look inside myself until the right words come out
And bring our love together.

SECOND CHANCE

I have love and I have lost love.

I have been in love and I have seen love walk away.

I have fallen in love and I have fallen out of love.

If I have the chance to love again as much as I like,

I would love a chance to love you again.

A HURTING HEART

A heart that is hurting can't see love or feel love.
A heart that is hurting says a lot of mean things.
A heart that is hurting tries to stop hurting by hurting itself.
A heart that is crying the pain of sorrow needs to wake up to a better tomorrow.
A heart that is hurting needs love and a desire to love.

This hurting hearts need you to love.

RATIONAL IN LOVE

Don't be a fool to love.

Love the one who wants to love you.

Give to the one who wants to give back.

Fall In love with someone who wants to fall in love with you.

Stay with the one who wants to stay with you.

See love for what it is and have a self-respecting love for yourself.

For love will love you when you least expect it.

But wait for it and don't be a fool to love.

I WILL LOVE AGAIN

You gave me a broken heart.
You have forsaken the vow of love you said to me.
You have taken my pain to a much higher level.
You have stolen my love and temporarily damaged it.
You have conveyed to me in so many ways,
That you just don't have love for me anymore.
But I will love again.
Because my love is unconditional and strong enough
To embrace someone who will love me back.
You may have broken my heart,
But not my passion for love . . .
It lives on.

LOST LOVE

What we had is gone,
And what we needed to survive
Was not enough.

We lost each other.
We lost our friendship with one another.
We lost our love for one another.

What we had is gone.
Why did we let go?

MY SILENT LOVE

My love:

It doesn't mean I don't love you just because I don't say it.
When I touch your heart,
I love you.

When I look into your eyes,
I love you.

When we are in each other dreams,
I love you.

When we are in each other's arms,
I love you.

When our lips meet in a sweet embrace,
I love you.

But the plain and simple fact is,
I do. Love you
Yes, so very much,

LETTING GO OF LOVE

Why do I let you hurt me?
Why do I take the pain you give?
Why do I never say anything?

Why do I never walk away from you?
Why do I hope for better days with you?
Why do I call what you do to me love?

Why? Because today, I no longer ask why;
For I know for myself that the love inside me deserves better.

So why don't I just relinquish all my thoughts of why,
And just say goodbye?

LOVE'S LOVE

Love took me over.
Love gave me joy and pain.
Love made my life so happy and yet so sad.

Love made me lie for the truth.
Love made me hurt but helped me to understand.
Love never let me forget what we had.
Love stayed in my heart and mind, and in my soul.

Love never let me go.
Love wants me to see that we love not for ourselves,
But for each other.

Love gave me humility and that made me a better lover.
Love took me over for all the right reasons;
Because love . . . loves me.

A SPECIAL NIGHT

Walking with you on the beach at night, my sweet.
The warm sand slipping through our toes ever so softly.
The moon glistens off the water and lay upon your eyes.
Your smile sparkles likes the stars at night.

We hold each other ever so tightly.
I look at you in the night and hope it enhances our love for one another even more.
Let the wave come rushing in upon us and flood our
Heart with a endless love like the ocean itself.

MUTUAL LOVE

Two hearts, one love,

Two views, one thought,

Two of us, one soul,

Two lives, one journey,

Two people in love, you and me,

One destiny . . . love infinity.

BETTER THAN A ROSE

Do I dare look upon this rose when I am looking at true beauty?
Do I let it fragrant lure my eyes away from you?
Why, when your sweet scent holds my heart?
Why do I want to give to you what you already possess?

Let it capture your beauty and scent only then it will know
Why my love could not be diverted from you.
What I see in you and what I feel for you
Is my love for you forever.

BEAUTIFUL

Are you the beauty that I've been looking for?
Are you the wonderful sight I've heard so much about?
Are you the song of delightment that rings in my heart?
If so, dazzle me with all that you have to give.

Let me know your sweet love.
Let me hold such beauty upon my eyes forever.
Let me look upon all that is you so that I may look no more
Let the picturesque view of you consume my heart with your love every time I look upon your enchanting beauty

VANITY

When the time comes when I don't call your name
anymore what will you do?
When the time comes when I don't love you anymore what
will you do?
When the time comes when I no longer crave for your
beauty what will you do?
When the time comes when I stop crying over you what
will you do?
When the time comes when your fragrance does not hold
my attention anymore,
what will you do?

You will miss this giving soul who just wanted to love you.
You will see vanity has no place in loving me.

AWAKEN BY YOUR LOVE

I can only dream of such a woman like you.
Your soft and gentle touch releases your very beauty.
Your caring eyes sparkles like the stars at night.
Your body is made up of a carnal delight.
Your mouth constantly speaks words of love.
Your affectionate ways overwhelm me.
My dream seem so real that I awake.
And only the thought of you lingers in my mind.
Then I awaken. I feel you reach for me.
Hello dream.

MY LOVE ALWAYS

My mind holds special thoughts of you.

My heart beats with love for you.

My love wants me to cuddle you in my arm.

My dreams become reality when you are in them.

My life awaits to spend eternity with you.

My eyes look upon the joy we can share together.

You mean more to me than you could ever know.

My love always.

WHY BE TOGETHER?

When is love wrong?
When we don't love each other any more?
When we can't talk to each other?
When we separate our bed?
When we are constantly hurting each other,
Emotionally and mentally?
When we're no longer feeling the need to hug or kiss?
When the lies continue to grow between us?

Loving you is wrong when we try to destroy each other's humanity.

NEED LOVE

I always look for this feeling we call love.
I always want to be in love.
I always felt the need to love.
I always talk about love.
I always want to live my life in love.
I always want to open my arms to love.
I always wanted to love that special someone.

Just to hold my sweetheart and love her always.

I PLEDGE MY LOVE

I am glad that we found love together.
We are so good together as true lovers.
We are so loving as we share and care for one another.
My heart is full of your love and I carry it with me always.
My life without you is unthinkable.

So here is my pledge to you . . .

Love you, love you, love you, kiss you and hug you, love you.
I'll just love you until the end of love's time.

A SWEET HELLO

Since that first hello you had my heart and more;
Since that first hello I thought of no one but you.
Why should I when all I want is you?
And that seems to be all that matters, then and now.
I did not tell my heart to stop beating . . . your hello did.
I did not tell my eyes to stare until they were engulfed by
your hello.
All I did was to love you and let you have my love.
Thank you for that sweet hello.

A SMILE FOR YOU

Have you ever seen this smile before?
This is my smile of my love for you.
From cheek to cheek this smile will brighten your everyday.
My smile wants you to fall in love with me.
This smile is for you only.
I hope it awakens in you the joy of my love for you.
I am smiling for you to enhance my love for you.
Give in to my smile and just smile back and love me.

MY OPEN LOVE

Here I am opening my heart to you,
Opening my love up to you,
And baring my soul to you.
My life can't bear another minute without you.
My words of love to you are honest and worthy of your love.
Can I be any more open about my love for you?
And how I want to cherish each day of my life with you?
Look at my love, its open to you.

CONFESSION OF LOVE

I am in love with you.
I will walk through the pain and fire of love just to be with you.
I will devour your entire negative thoughts about loving me
Just to be with you.

I would deprive you of nothing about love if you just give your love to me.
I want to be with you.
I would give you my entire love without any hesitation just to be with you.
I would devote every loving moment showing you how much I really love you.
Yes, I am in love with you.

PRICELESS

Exquisite as the very night,

Priceless as a fine jewel,

Captivating loveliness to your very soul.

Arousing enchanting beauty that stands before my eyes,

Charming yet elegant love that entrapped my heart.

I see your sensitive and caring way reach out to me,

As well as your warmth and understanding that holds me

All of it in my hand where I polish you until your love brightened my life

With your rare love.

GIFT OF LOVE

I remember all the love we gave to each other

The memories are so etch in my mind
You gave me so much to remember about us being in love
That until this day I still love you
Every time I picture your beauty in my mind
It leaves me longing for our love again
I know I will never forget your gift of love
Thank you for leaving these impressions of love
Etched in my mind

MY LOVE IS YOU

My quest for love leads me to you.

My yearning for love said it had to be you.

My dreams saw the face of love and it was you.

My heart was touched by love and it had your soft touch.

Are you my undying love?

For I am here for you to love.

GAME OF LOVE

When you play games in love, you will always lose in love
So stop pretending that you don't love me
Don't look away when I look at you
Let your words flood my heart with loving passion
Other than sour misgivings
You can see how I show my love for you
Stop the games of love before you get hurt by losing my love
Don't miss the chance to love me

HOW MUCH I LOVE YOU

Oh, I love you so much!

Every time I look at you, I realize love gave you to me to cherish.

I do so with the understanding that we are forever in love with each other.

We will cultivate our love into what we are and what we mean to each other,

And what we devote ourselves to as two people in love with one another.

I love you and I love us together . . . that's how much I love you.

A PLACE IN MY HEART

Your beauty surpasses the depth of my heart.
You have the sensual glow of soft candlelight.

Your personality surpasses that of a brilliant love.
I know you and I know your love.
It makes me want you, need you, and desire you.
Your love fills me with an overwhelming love that's
Cherishable only by your sweet smile.

I am glad I captured this moment of love with you,
Because now I am not deprived of such a enchanting beauty
That I won't let go.

LET OUR LOVE SOAR

I care for you, can't you feel me?
I keep your love in my heart.
Entrust all that I say to you.
Please know that I love you with every beat of my heart.
I ascend into your life for many reasons.
One is that I may savor your love.
The very delight of your love uplifts me to your beauty
that I keep with me
Knowing how much I love you.

YOU LEFT ME

You left me tingling all over,
You left me grasping for air,
You left me licking my lips for your sweet juicy,
You left me bursting with passion,
You left me longing for more of your love,
You left me quivering for your love,

After all of that, you left me passed out on the floor.

LOVE DREAMS

Lay your head in my arms and let me sing you to sleep

With a song of passion and desire to keep.

A song of sweet exquisite intimacy between us.

A song that will capture your imagination to love.

Close your eyes and hold on to love's fantasy and me

For this song will unfold into our reality.

Just sleep my love and let each word I sing hold you and

Bring us ever close to love's dream.

ONE IN A CROWD

Out of a crowd, I found you to love.
Everyday since that day, you have done nothing to
disappoint me in loving you.
I am so happy that you were in that crowd for me;
Because when my heart took that glance at you,
It never let you go.
I knew then you were mine forever.

The completion for the love of my life discontinued with
that look,
And my destiny of love unfolded into love
Happily ever after.

WHILE YOU'RE ASLEEP

While you lay down and are asleep,
I watch over your beauty.
I look at you until my eyes weep as well as my heart.
I can't believe you chose me to love.

Someone so beautiful and yet quite extraordinary
I see so much wonder in you that I can't explain, nor do I want to.
For as long as you are with me, laying in our bed
I just want to look upon your beauty tonight and always.

Thank God for your love that sleeps upon this pillow and my heart.

EROTICA

I want so badly to love you passionately.

I like to feel me inside of you.

I want so badly to taste your sexy body until you . . .

I want so badly to make love to you everyday in so many ways.

I want so badly to kiss your succulent lips and feel your tongue inside my mouth

I want so badly to sleep with you and hold your naked body next to mine.

I want so badly to consume your sweet juice on my tongue.

You should know how much I really want you so badly, my love.

AFTER THE RAIN

It rained in my heart today.
First light drizzle that mists all over our love,
Then the steady rain that cover our body with a new life of love,
Then a heavy downpour and wind blowing rains all about us.
As we hold each other ever so tightly.

Embracing the rain and our love for one another,
The rain comes to an end as we stand together.
I can see the rain coming down your face.
Raindrops pass your glittering eyes to your soft warm lips
And I long to kiss each raindrop
Suddenly a rainbow wrap us up in it love forever.

NEVER STOP LOVING YOU

This is the pinnacle of my life.
Your love lingers as the most enchanting
Yet delicate sweet thought that passes through my heart
My love is still devoted to you.
There might have been other loves,
But I deceive my own self
And in doing so, I lose your love.
Sadness runs through my heart until this day.
Longing still to love you . . . just you.
That thirst will never leave me.
My heart will continue to ache for your love

CRY

I cry.
I cried when you said goodbye.
I cried when you stopped loving me.
I cried with the last kiss on your lips.

I cry because I am too sad to live my life without you.
I cry late at night just before I close me eyes.
I cry for you.

I cry and the teardrops roll down my face
And I know that is goodbye . . .
But I still cry.

BEFORE IT'S TOO LATE

I never wanted to walk away from you or to lose sight of
what we have
I thought together meant together
Let us not fall into a long separation
That we may not lose all that we gather in love
I don't wont to walk away from you now or ever
All I want is to stay with you and give you the love I
promise
Please walk with me not away from me

UNDYING LOVE FOR YOU

I have loved you like no other,
Now I can die happy.
I have cherished you like a sweet flower,
Now I can die happy.
Your fragrant of love still lingers around me even at this moment,
Now I can die happy.
You have satisfied my craving desire for loving you,
Now I can die happy.

I look upon your beauty for the last time and pray that it never leaves my heart or mind
For all I know is your love.
It was my life dream come true.
Now death has come and I can die happy knowing that I loved you.
Goodbye my love.

YOU WALKED IN

I let you walk in to my life to love you.

I let you see how frantic I was to love you.

I was not so graceful and stumbled with my love for you.

I not only want your love but your friendship as well to cherish.

You may think walking in to my love was a wonderful thing, and it might be.

But you walk in because of my love you.

WE CAN ONLY GET BETTER

My love is not a prefect love.

I don't always say I love you.

I don't always kiss you.

I don't always listen to you.

I don't always fulfill your needs.

I don't always say the right things at the right time.

But in loving you I will always try to get better at loving you.

WHILE YOU WERE WAITING

While you were waiting to love me, I found someone else.

She held my hand and said the words "I love you."

And the ways she looks at me fills me with passion

She did not make me wait for her love,

She just gave it to me.

She loved me.

Without any hesitation

LOVE IN REVERSE

Let our last time be our first
Let's say goodbye but than say hello
Let me hold you where you stand but never let you go
Let our too night always brighten each day
Let my like for you turn into everlasting love for you
If this love could have a beginning that would never end
So would my love than be forever

YOU ARE MY LOVE

Why does love call your name to me?

Does it not know your name is always upon my lips?

That my heart leaps at the sound of your sweet name?

If I shall hear another name it would not compare to your delicate name?

Let love call your name to me that its gentile breeze may incite me to whisper it back

And surrender myself to your love.

ALWAYS TOGETHER

I shall never stop loving you.

I will always need you.

I need to share my life with you.

I have a great respect for you.

I see us as one for each other.

As long as we have each other, our love will constantly grow.

We will never part, not even in death.

GIVE TO ME

Give me the wings to fly into your life.

Give me the passion to grab you and never let you go.

Give me your arms that I may wrap them around me

And nestle myself so gently into your warm body.

Give to me all your enticing love

That I may quench my thirst of my love for you.

TOSSING MY HEART

I throw my heart to you.
I throw my soul to you.
I throw myself to you.
I throw my understanding to you.
I throw my feelings to you.
I throw my devotion to you.
I throw my love to you.

Not even a hurricane can find its way to your love.
Just surrender your love to me.
Don't repel my love for you.
Let it come through for it will only caress
Your heart with the magic of my love for you.

A MIRROR IMAGE

When I look into the mirror, I see myself as a hopeful romantic.

I see myself longing to love,

I see myself yearning for love,

I see myself fragile to love,

I see myself sensitive to love,

I see myself loving to give hugs and kisses to someone,

I see the face of my love changing for the best,

And yet I just see me.

ENCHANTING BEAUTY

I see all the beauty that stands before me
And my eyes I can't bare its intoxicating beauty
For it engulfs me and dares me to look away
For a moment, but I can't.

Your beauty has enticed me to love you.
Your alluring beauty called to me to look upon it
And give myself to you.
I am in ecstasy forever over you sweet radiant beauty.

THOSE SPECIAL MOMENTS

I am reminded of the special moments in which we share our love for each other.

Like the silent sunrise we share its loving warmth.

Like the loving word we spoke to each other.

Like the long deep loving stare into each other eyes that seem to last forever.

Like how each touch awakens love in the both of us.

I am so aroused by all the special moments we had together

Because if we had nothing else, we had love for one another.

Those were special moments that we will never forget.

WILL YOU?

Will you have me to love?

Will you devote your love to me?

Will you give me a chance to love you?

Will you see what makes me, me?

Will you compromise in love with me?

Will you see this love through the very end?

Will you?

YOUR WAY OF LOVE

makes me tremble.

The way you love, loves me and makes me bashful.

The way you love, loves me and makes me blissful.

The way you love, loves me and makes me excited.

The way you love, feels like love.

A MESSAGE FROM LOVE

Love walked out of my life.

Maybe love wanted to show me something.

What an awful feeling this is to have.

When love walked out I was so bewildered by how love hurt me.

Must I know the pain of love to be a better lover?

Or must I respect loves misery to grow stronger in my life

Or be submissive to love coming and going?

ONLY ME

Give to me what you gave to no other.

Say to me the words no one else has heard.

Pleasure me that I am still weakened by your love.

Hold me as if this is our final goodbye.

Share my life as new so we can walk together lovingly.

Share with me your love that you may never share it with anyone except me.

IF ONLY

If I never let you go,
If I never stop kissing you,
If I never stop calling your name in love,
If I never stop holding you with passion,
If I never, ever again love someone as lovely as you,
If I never see happiness when I know that I am fortunate
to have you to love,

Because I can only love you.

MY VOW

My vow to you is to love you.
Is to always talk to you.
Is to always listen to you.
Is to be there for you.
Is to keep you from harm.
Is to comfort you always.
Is to say the wonderful things I said to get you.
Is to love you as my friend as well as my wife.
Is to give you the very best that my life has to offer.
Is to never put anyone before you -- ever.
Is to never let my heart forget you at anytime in my life.
This is my loving vow to you.

LOVE

Love . . . love . . . love . . .
Love you
Love me
Love us
Love life
Love one other
Love god.

Love holds us in its heart and mind;
To let us see how far we can give of ourselves to one
another
In love

JOYOUS LOVE

I am so happy with you.
I am so happy we met.
I am so happy we fell in love.
I am so happy we kiss.

I am so happy we can enjoy life together.
I am so happy just to lay down and wake up next to you each day.
I am so happy that we are together forever my love

Yes, I am so happy to have you in my life;
Because, without you, my happiness would just go away.

A LOVE SONG

Sing to me a love song of deep passion
With words that let me feel you touching my soul.
Let it arouse in me the joy of my love for you.

Let your voice sing out with your devotion for our love
Let's have meaning beyond meaning.
Sing so I may be overcome with ecstasy
That it may excite me to merge our bodies together with
just a glance.

May the intensity of the song linger in our hearts forever.

GIVE TO ME

Do you hold that what is precious to me in your heart?

Why don't you give to me your love that I truly deserve?

Entrust in me your exquisite rare beauty

That I may hold it up to the moon itself so it may dazzle the stars.

Entrap not only my heart, but also my very existence.

Let me love you until the sun comes up a thousand times or more.

What a pure delight our love could be when you give your heart to love.

REFLECTIONS

When I think of you,
I think of how you've made such a difference in my life.
You have given me so much to look forward to.

As I reflect on my memories of today,
And it's meaning,
And what lies ahead for us tomorrow,
I look forward to a new "us," constantly changing in love.

A LOVER'S DREAM

A lover's dream is to dream of love.
A lover's dream is what he sees.
A lover's dream is to be a romantic lover.
A lover's dream is his love's dream come true.
A lover dream is to love outside his dream.

We can dream of many things,
Why not dream of love and loving you?

WHAT HAVE WE HERE?

Have I stumbled upon your love that's hidden deep inside of you?

Have I spoken words of love that have unlocked the passion you have kept inside of you?

Have I looked into your eyes and met your soul singing a love song of ecstasy?

Have I touched in you the craving for love that you want and need to give to someone?

Or have they always been there and I am the first to unleash its desire inside of you?

Surrender you love to me that I may love you for the first time

And give to you the romantic life you deserve.

WHAT WILL IT TAKE?

If I tear down the great wall to get to you,

If I climb the highest mountain to get to you,

If I sail across every ocean just to get to you,

If I cross the widest desert just to get to you,

What if I just pick a rose and gave it to you?

Can I than stop my adventure of love where we now stand

And spend the rest of my day loving you?

CAN I?

I love you but can I be what you want me to be?

Can I look at you the way you want me to?

Can I give to you the joy you deserve?

Do I make love to you with the passion and warmth you desire?

I hold what we have as the most important thing in my life.

Help me give to you, show to you, and say to you, everyday

That yes, I do love as much, if not even more than life itself.

LET'S LOVE TOMORROW

Maybe tomorrow will be a better day to be in love.
So hold your feelings for today, and do not disturb our love
For tomorrow we will be in love forever.
So let's embrace tomorrow's love.

ONE SWEET LOVE

One sweet kiss that will last forever,
One sweet embrace that will bring us closer to forever,
One sweet delightful smile that will brighten up this room,
One sweet sensual night that will stay forever,
One sweet you that I will share my life with,
One sweet word that will say it all . . .

Love.

HERE'S MY LOVE

I call your name but you don't respond.
I reach for your hand and you take it away.
I say I love you and you ignore me and my love.

I want so much to be with you,
But the distance you keep between us is too much.
Here I am love me,
As I want to love you.
Give to me as I give to you.
If love is what you want;
Then here I stand wanting for you to love me,
So that I can love you back.

LOOK WHAT YOU'VE DONE

You smile at me and you have given me a glimmer of hope to love you.

You have opened your heart to all my sweet thoughts of you.

You helped me to see a greater love that stimulates my life.

I have not found this love that you possess in anyone else.

My love can look upon you and forever see your smile.

Your very beauty captivates all that I want to do . . . just to love.

FOOTSTEPS

Walk into my love and see the bright colors of my life fill you with enormous joy.

Walk into my mind and let your thoughts engulf me in the mystery of my love for you.

Walk into my heart and let its rhythm sway you to love me even more.

Walk into my love and never walk away.

LAUGHTER

Laughter helps my soul.
Laughter helps my mind.
Laughter helps my life.
Laughter helps my pain.
Laughter helps my love for you.
Laughter helps my loneliness.
Laughter helps my todays and tomorrows.

Laughter walks with me as a helper
That won't let me down because it's too busy;
Keeping me laughing at myself and my life.

Have you laughed out loud today?

IMAGES OF YOU

I keep a picture of your radiant beauty near my bed.

I see it every day but this picture is not enough to love.

I am grateful for how it keeps your love etched in my heart.

I look upon it and kiss your love in my mind.

I see it and I realize why I want this picture of you in my thoughts and dreams.

Because I love to be with you each day.

That's why your picture is by my bed.

LOVE LYRICS

Let me pour my love lyrics upon you.
Listen to my words of love.
Let them move you to hug someone, kiss someone,
especialy to love someone.
Feel the rhythm flow throughout you body.
Feel the passion move you to be a lover.

Reach out to love your father, mother, daughter, son, wife,
husband, and friend.
Remember, the best feeling you could ever have is the
feeling of giving your love.
Let's speak of love.
Let's sing of love.
Let's demonstrate love and give nothing to chance.

Love is who you are and what you can become.
It is free to give and you have it always.
So reach out in love.
Stand out as a lover, for if you love today,
Life will love you tomorrow.
I love you . . .

ROMANTIC EVENING

A candle lit for us.
The bath is waiting for us.
Chilled drinks waiting for us.
Soft music for just us.
Love is in the air for us.

This sequence is not a dream,
This is my life of romance that I would love to share
With you, always. Come share this romantic evening with
me.

KISS ME

Your kiss, your sweet loving kiss . . .
The touch of your lips against mine leaves me quivering all over
With a loving sensation that has me longing for you.
Your succulent, ripe, juicy lips pressed against mine
Finds my tongue passionately feeling the warmth of your love.

Please kiss my lips.
That's all I want and care to remember.
Oh, darling, so warm are your kisses.
Let each kiss touch my heart once more in a loving way.
Kiss me.

THANK YOU

I thank you for always being there for me.
I thank you for the best time of my life.
I thank you for your unconditional love.
I thank you for the passion that I still feel.
I thank you for all the sunshine you put upon my heart.
I thank you for the journey of loving you.
I thank you for your alluring smile that captivates my soul.

Thanks for loving me is not enough to say
To someone who loves you with their all.
But from the bottom of my heart . . .
Thank you.

LOVE'S INFINITY

I plan to love you for a long time.
I plan to better us as husband and wife.
I will give to you my fidelity.
I will give to you godly love.
I will give to you a life of sweet memories.
You will be what you are to me the day I met you.

Today when I marry you with my unconditional love,
We will have the most priceless and precious love in life.
I hold your hand today and I plan to never let it go.
I am proud of this day in my life for I found you to share it with forever.
My tears of joy is my baptism into loving you,
And only you shall I love until infinity.

LOVE BEFORE DEATH

Before you die,
You are given a life to live your journey.
You have given much love to your family and friends
You have touched the lives of so many.

I miss you now and you have not left yet.
I don't want you to go,
But somehow I know you'll be better off.
I don't think I will be after you leave.
The best part of knowing you and loving you
Is that what you gave . . . simply you.

Even though you are leaving,
The memory will stay in my heart.
So when I am sad and missing you,
My heart brings up all the wonderful times we shared together.
I can truly say you made an enormous difference in my life.

May God stay close to you.
For you will always be close in my heart,

Before you die . . .
I love you.

ONLY IF

If life only gave me one thing it was you to love
If you only gave me one thing to have it was your heart
If I have one thing to give back to you it would be my unconditional love
If one love is all I need in my life I am happy to say it would be you
If love in our lives is what we have then our love will last forever, as one, as long as we share our lives of love and dreams together in our heart
We will be one

MY SIMPLE LOVE

My heart is a meek one when it come to my love for you
I am submissive to your modest ways in which you give your love to me
Degrading your love is not but it is so uplifting I will admit I am a coward when you are in my presence, bashful at best
Oh my honorable love I respectfully humble my heart for you to love
Subdue me in my lowly hours and let my loyalty bring forth my plan and simple love for you
Shame you I will not but let my polite word say to you how humble I am to stand before you
Loving you all my days long
Loving you, I say, all my days long

I FOUND LOVE IN YOU

I've found courage in loving you
I found all the joy I needed in loving you
You saw my pain and made my love strong
My love was wrapped up inside of me and you set it free
Just by being my friend to love
I've found love when I found you to love in my life

TWO KINDS OF LOVE

There are only two kinds of love that
I want to remember in my life

My first is with you
and the moments we share

And

My last is with you now
and the life we have.

I love you

About the Author

    I'm a hopeless romantic with the desire to always share passion and the love that is within me to give. Yes I am that person who likes beautiful walks on the beach, great conversation, and candlelight dinners while gazing into your beautiful eyes, saying the words that will light up your heart and soul. I am the one who would love to cuddle with you on the couch in front of a fireplace. I am that person who wants to share the words really deep down inside of our hearts together. That is what I'm about and that's who I am.

    Please read this book and feel the passion above that *Love Lyrics* can do with your heart and soul and mind.

www.ingramcontent.com/pod-product-compliance
Lightning Source LLC
Chambersburg PA
CBHW021428070526
44577CB00001B/105